I Would Lick It For Hours
Two Lumps-Year One

Mel Hynes and J. Grant

Stonegarden.net Publishing
http://www.stonegarden.net

Reading from a different angle.

I Would Lick It For Hours: Two Lumps-Year One Copyright © 2007 Mel Hynes and James L. Grant

ISBN: 1-60076-119-4

This is a work of fiction. Names, characters, places and incidents are products of the author's imagination or are used fictitiously and are not to be construed as real. Any resemblance to actual events, locales organizations or persons, living or dead, is entirely coincidental.

StoneGarden.net Publishing
3851 Cottonwood Dr.
Danville, CA 94506

All rights reserved. Printed in the United States of America. No part of this book may be used or reproduced in any manner whatsoever without written permission, except in the case of brief quotations embodied in critical articles and reviews. For information address StoneGarden.net Publishing.

First StoneGarden.net Publishing paperback printing:
November 2007

Visit StoneGarden.net Publishing on the web at http://www.stonegarden.net.

See The Lumps at: http://www.twolumps.net

I WOULD LICK IT FOR HOURS

TWO LUMPS - YEAR ONE

By Mel Hynes and J. Grant

INTRODUCTION

I am not a cat person. My boyfriend has a cat, and it is his baby. The cat and I tolerate one another. There are millions of people who treat their cats like children. Small fluffy children who can't file law suits. There are billions of photos online of cute kittens with wide eyes. Thousands of websites devoted to the adorableness of cats. There are cartoons that worship the cuddliness of felines. This is not one of those cartoons.

Cats are sometimes dumb, mostly evil, and they own us. Cats have evolved to the point where they have figured out how to get their pets to work for them beyond fetch and sit. We feed them, brush them, scoop their shit, and buy toys that they're not interested in. All this so that we can be ignored and toyed with by them. And we love them for it.

Two Lumps is a comic about cats as they are. Sometimes they're idiots, sometimes they're cute, but usually they're devious fur balls. They get their eyeballs stuck under bathroom doors, run around the house for no apparent reason, and watch us in the bathroom. Two Lumps is *Calvin and Hobbes* childlike insanity. It's *Garfield* on meth.

Plenty of cartoons have explored the eccentricities of cats. Yes, they chase their tails. Yes, they lick their butts. But they also drink vodka and compose sonnets. If you have two cats, then you know Ebenezer and Snooch. The criminal mastermind and the fat, lovable idiot. Hell, if you have siblings then you know these two. One sibling dares the other to jump off the roof with a pillowcase as a parachute. Somehow the fact that they're telepathic cats doesn't hinder the fact that we all know someone just like these two fur balls. I can't tell you that this is a comic about two overweight cats because that would conjure up far too many stereotypes. This is a comic about the devious idiots that we all know in our lives. Our childhood, our innocence, and the psychotic mayhem that it all was and always will be.

Jennie Breeden is the creator of the world-famous comic The Devil's Panties (which really isn't satanic porn). She wears stompy boots and likes pirates and men in kilts. Visit her on the web at **www.thedevilspanties.com**

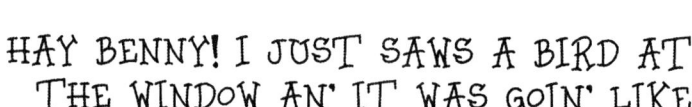

ARTIST'S NOTE: Thus began my foray back into webcomics after a year hiatus! I was so ready to get in that saddle again. I had the plan, I had the wherewithal, everything was groovy!

ARTIST'S NOTE: We have made fun of Garfield since the beginning.

The sulkiness of a cat can be measured by their height in relation to their width.

Slight sulk

Half sulk

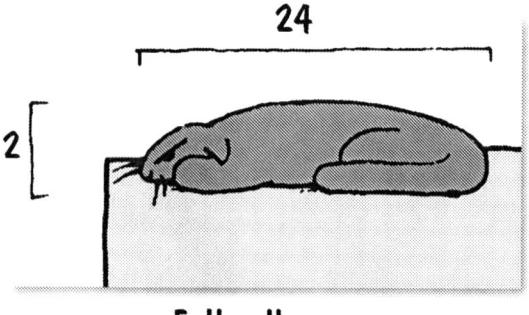

Full sulk

```
WRITER'S NOTE: It's always fascinated me how a 20-pound cat can
     flatten himself into an emo-puddle two inches thick.
```

WRRRRRRRRRRRRRRRRRRRR

MOW.

It's just a can of green beans, Snooch. Not gooshyfood.

MOW!

Green beans, dammit!

```
WRITER'S NOTE: ...and when you GIVE them a bean to prove it, they
        glare like you conjured it from the void.
```

Cats are capable of holding entire conversations via tail-twitching motions. Observe:

What we see

Translated

ARTIST'S NOTE: Our cats can hold entire debates using three inches of tail each.

WRITER'S NOTE: I think this is why they attack twitching string so fiercely. We see a cute toy, but in cat-butt semaphore it's saying rude things about their mother.

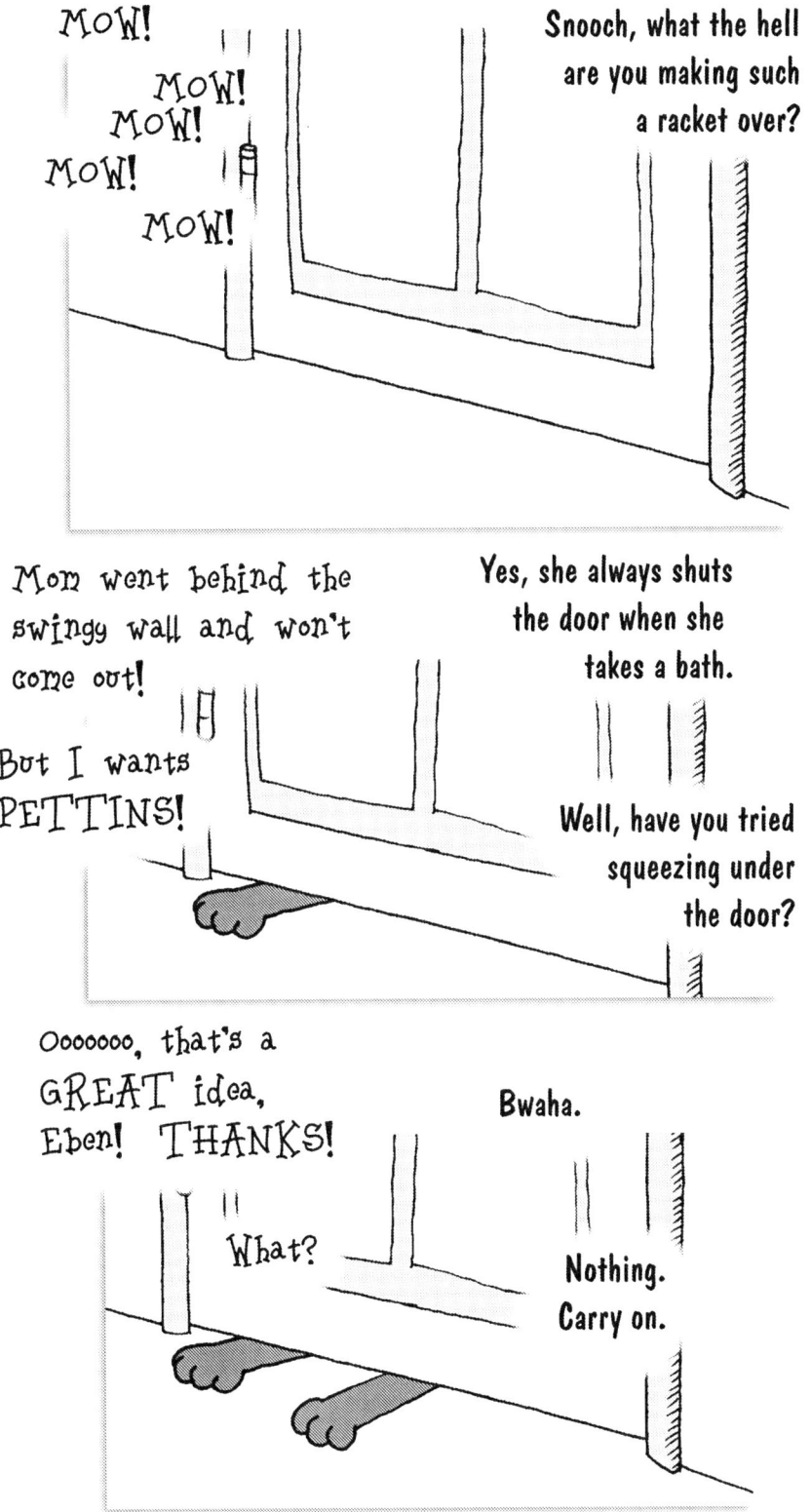

WRITER'S NOTE: This was inspired by the real-life "Snooch" trying to squeeze under the bedroom door.

WRITER'S NOTE: There was the typical muffled "mow mow mow" outside, then a sudden "MOW!" that sounded like it was in the room.

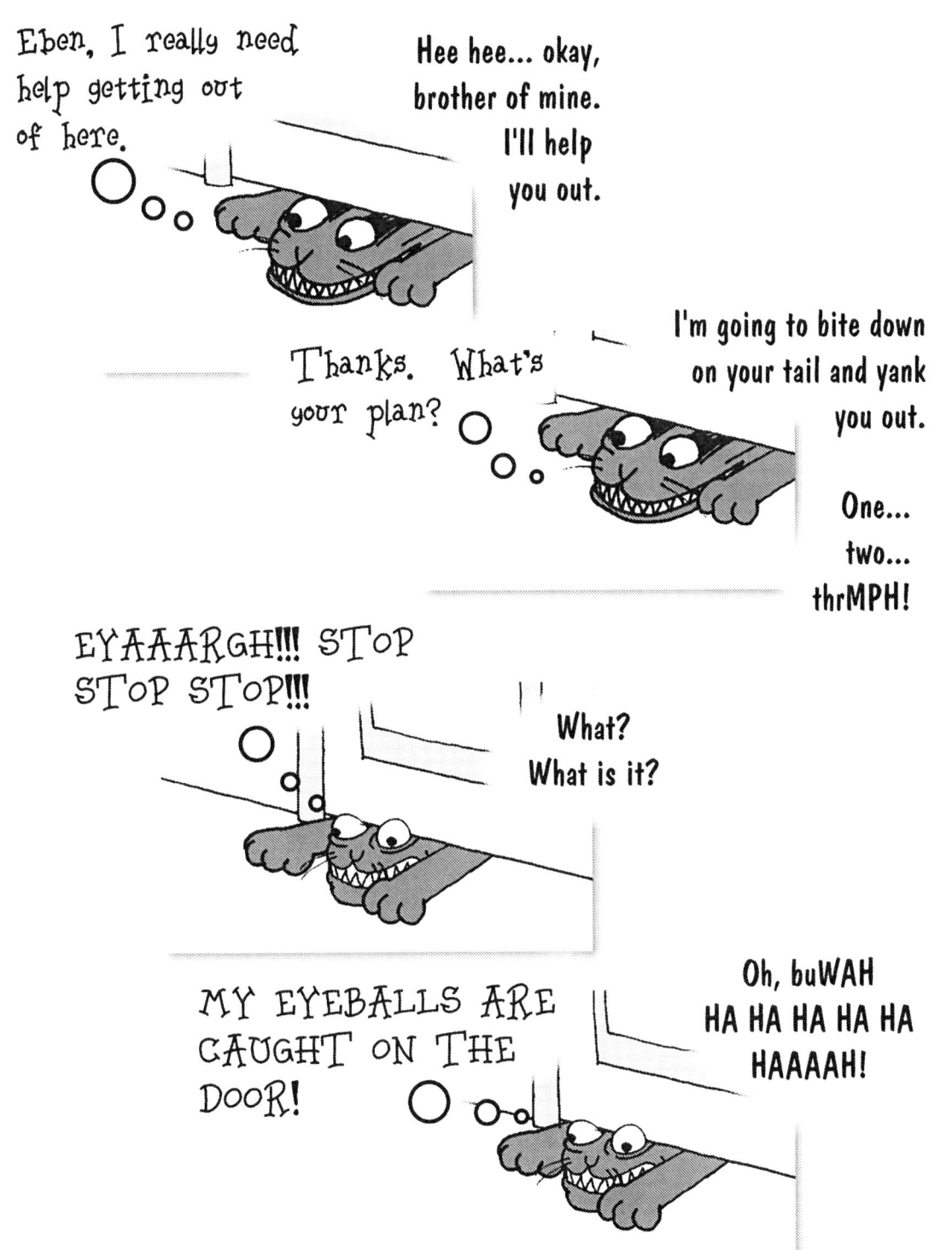

WRITER'S NOTE: Looking over, he'd managed to shove his nose, one ear, two legs and the end of his tail through the crack sideways.

WRITER'S NOTE: It was the most pathetic attempt at feline limbo ever.

> Oh boy!
> Lasagna!
> I love lasagna!

> Oh boy!
> 50 pounds of Chili! I love 50 pounds of chili!

> Oh boy!
> Cement!

> Pig? Or *retarded pig?* You decide!

ARTIST'S NOTE: Someday I will do battle hand-to-hand with Jim Davis and eat his entrails.

WRITER'S NOTE: This story arc is actually what started the entire strip.

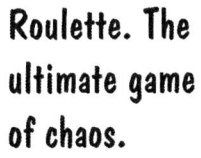  

WRITER'S NOTE: We were in Reno, indulging in the free drinks, and started discussing what it would be like if my cats were gambling.

ARTIST'S NOTE: I remember distinctly that one of my first concepts was her dumber cat calling the Double Zero the "Oooooo."

WRITER'S NOTE: Several hours of hysteria later, J. insisted he "had to make this into a new comic. Nothing big, just 3 or 4 of them."

```
ARTIST'S NOTE: I have no idea why cats do this.  My theory presented
              here makes as much sense as any other.

WRITER'S NOTE: I disagree, only because the NASDAQ is closed at 3 AM
              when they usually do this.
```

WRITER'S NOTE: This, on the other hand, I fully agree with.

ARTIST'S NOTE: We did not often use profanity in Two Lumps as each time we did resulted in much angry fan mail.

WRITER'S NOTE: The love mail from fellow Monkey Island fans helped make up for it, though.

Eben, why are you in here? I'm bathing!

CAT'S LOG, STARDATE 24056.8: I have finally discovered how these creatures wash themselves, and it's not a sight for the squeamish.

These "humans" lack proper tongues for washing, and have to make do with synthetic, cloth-based ones...

Not now, Snooch.

HEY, BENNY! I got a MAGIC TRICK to show you!

I can make you all soapy by waving my paw!

SNOOCH! NO!!!

What the deuce are you... hey! cut that out, fleabag!

BAT BAT BAT

SPLOOSH!

HEE HEE HEE HEE
DIE DIE DIE DIE

WRITER'S NOTE: My doctor keeps asking me how I get these lacerations. I don't think she believes me, which proves she doesn't have a cat.

WRITER'S NOTE: Cats aren't much different from kids in this regard. Or college students. Or J.

BAD TIMING FOR A FART

ARTIST'S NOTE: This strip had to be redrawn from scratch for its inclusion into this book. The original was done in ten minutes, drawn directly with a mouse and posted willy-nilly to the site. It would have looked ridiculous in proper print format.

WRITER'S NOTE: I've always used this as the argument against people who say housecats have an ideal life. Your tongue is your toilet paper.

WRITER'S NOTE: This is one of our best-known strips. I think everyone who's been around a cat knows the pitiful wibbling noise they make at the window when birds appear.

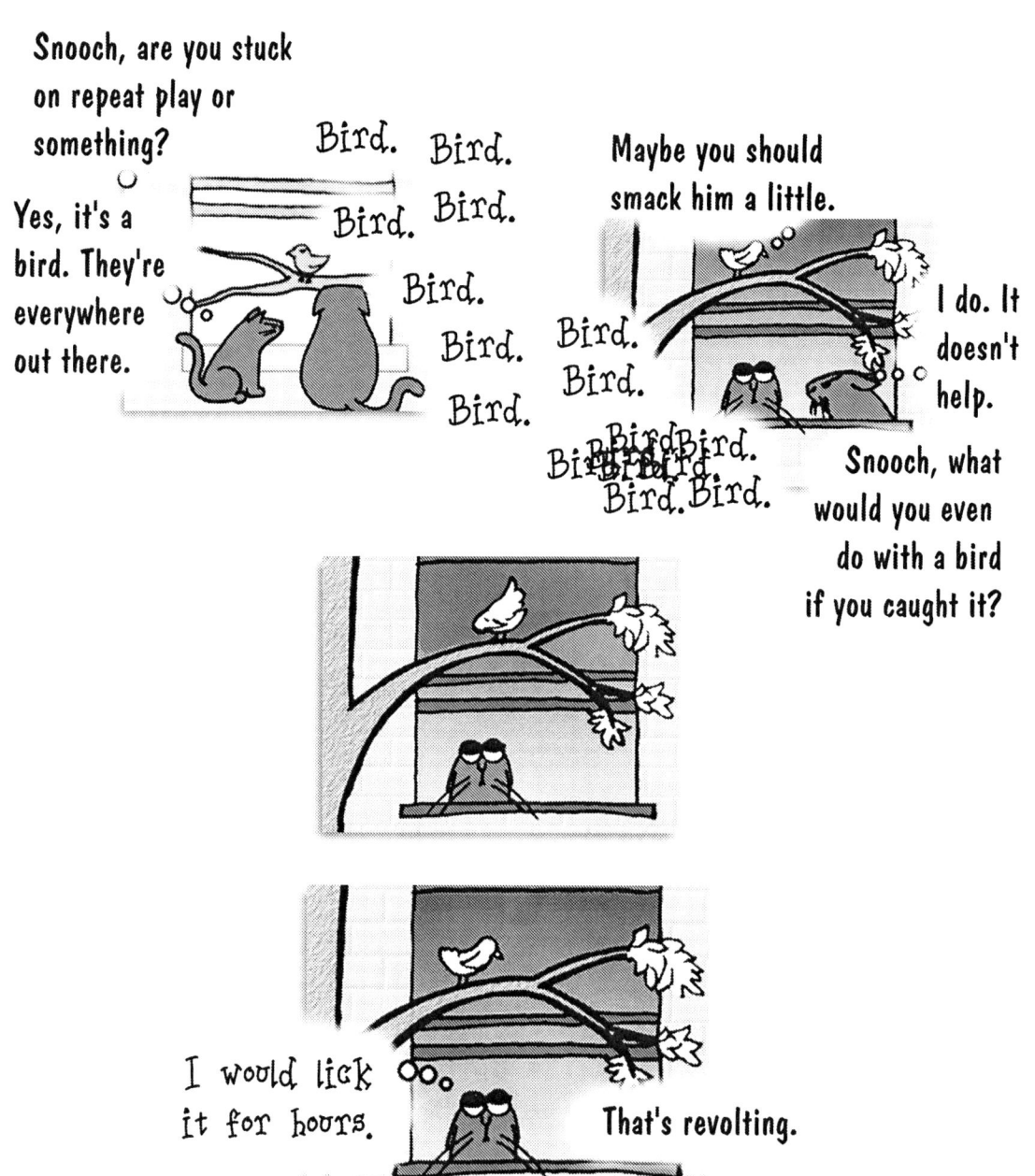

WRITER'S NOTE: One of my childhood cats was not fully up on the whole idea of "hunting". He would catch birds and have no idea what to do with them, so he'd bring them into the house and let them go. It made my Mom nuts.

AND NOW, EBEN AND SNOOCH IN: SUPER HAPPY CHIBI FUN TIME CIRCUIT NEKO TIME!

ARTIST'S NOTE: We do these whenever we get invited to an anime convention.

WRITER'S NOTE: Neko Neko Waargh.

I'm gonna getcha, oooh, you dead, gonna getcha...

Snooch, how did you get up on the bookshelf?

DEATH FROM ABOVE!

CRASH

Your attack on the linoleum was quite impressive there, chief.

Owie.

WRITER'S NOTE: "Eben" actually pulled this one, madly flailing his way into a group of guests. His ego has never recovered.

WRITER'S NOTE: Cats obsess about messing with the strangest things. Ours try to destroy knitting, tools, and David Duchovny.

ARTIST'S NOTE: Poor David.

WRITER'S NOTE: This is obviously a California roach, as it's smaller than Snooch.

WRITER'S NOTE: This was the most hysterically awful gift "Snooch" ever brought me. He was so proud of his hunting skills, too.

ARTIST'S NOTE: Sometimes "Snooch" really does seem to confuse his brother for a rodent.

ARTIST'S NOTE: The first appearance of Meer! This is "Snooch's" real-life noise of impatient disapproval.

WRITER'S NOTE: It killed me when the vet told me "Snooch" needed Small Dog sized doses of medication because he was so large. They're both actually on a carefully monitored diet, but he remains a chunkbutt no matter what the vet and I try. But he's healthy and happy, at least.

WRITER'S NOTE: Ah, the 15-minute scraping sessions of derision.

I looked and I saw him,
The Dork in the Bonnet.

WRITER'S NOTE: A fan actually sent us email on why the (utterly made-up) equation is invalid, and a correction for it. I'm not sure if I'm impressed or terrified.

No matter where I go in the room, your butt seems to follow me.

ARTIST'S NOTE: Trompe that Oeil!

(sung to Superman's theme.)

WRITER'S NOTE: There's also the "Kitty Banjo" song. Don't ask.

ARTIST'S NOTE: A friend of ours insists that all intelligent people sing songs to their cats. She may be onto something.

ARTIST'S NOTE: Possibly *the* most popular strip we've ever done.

WRITER'S NOTE: Scratch the "possibly".

ARTIST'S NOTE: I could be wrong, but I believe at this point Mel was writing the strip full time.

WRITER'S NOTE: We were in transition at this point. You can tell which are mine by the "I haven't got the hang of this yet" bulk of dialogue.

WRITER'S NOTE: This was when we were still in a second-floor apartment. The neighbor's tiny pug (about the size of "Snooch") mistakenly wandered in a couple of times, causing mass confusion over a dog that was smaller than they were.

WHY WE NEVER HEAR ABOUT THE CATS OF WAR

WRITER'S NOTE: They do have a point.

WRITER'S NOTE: This was my first real story arc. And it's 100% true. I think it's a legend in the vet's office.

WRITER'S NOTE: Putting both cats in a dog carrier seemed like SUCH a brilliant idea on paper.

Ugh... hey, we stopped moving.

Thank the powers that be.

What's that bizarre odor? Smells like... *dogs?*

Teh big mouses?

Don't even start about food after what you just did, Snooch. I've been tackled, flung around in this box and puked on. My only consolation is that this day can only get better.

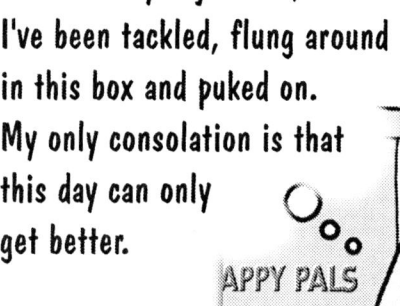

APPY PALS ETERINARY CLINIC

```
WRITER'S NOTE: At the time, I was thinking "At least they've gotten it
                out of their system..."
```

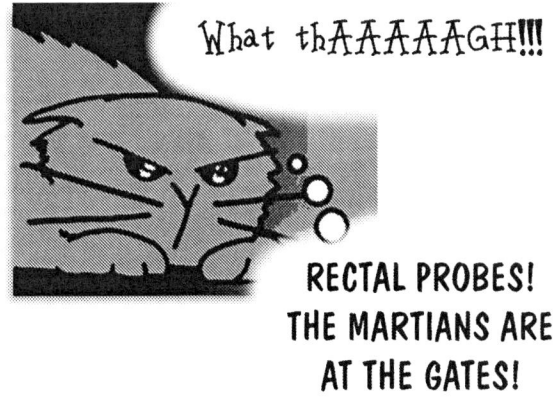

WRITER'S NOTE: I've always wondered if alien abductions are just interplanetary vets. They kidnap you, give you shots and stick things in your butt. We should recognize this routine!

OK, now we just need a blood sample...

AAAAAAAAAUGH!!!

Next they'll attempt to dissect him for study! WE HAVE TO ESCAPE!

RARRRRR!

And these are your shots... OW! Nurse, can you hold him?

Yes, Snooch! FIGHT! We must make a noble stand against the Martian invaders!

FIGHT! YOU'VE NEVER BEEN SMART ENOUGH TO GIVE UP ON ANYTHING BEFORE! NOW FIGHT, DAMN YOU! FIGHT!

whew All done! Ebenezer, it's your turn!

My brother is compromised... maybe they won't want a dead specimen.

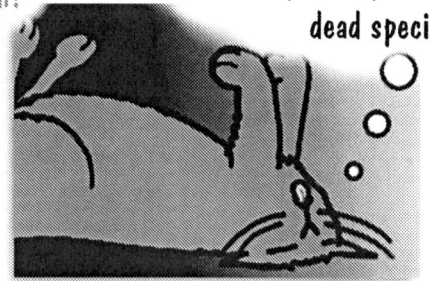

WRITER'S NOTE: "Snooch" does spaz at the vet the second they start prodding him. "Eben", however, relies on passive resistance by going completely limp.

Nurse, it appears Ebenezer is playing dead again.

"Again?" Fool! I've never been here before!

...Or *have* I?

I'll just leave him here. Seems he and his brother have put on weight again.

SWEET CREAM! They've done this before! I must be suffering from alien-induced amnesia!

Stay calm, Eben. Don't break character.

WHUMP

Man, that's some "dead weight!" HA HA HA!

Laugh it up, Martian. Your time will come, so help me...

WRITER'S BLOCK: He's also a "hysterical shedder", meaning he turns into the cat version of a spore-bursting mushroom.

WRITER'S NOTE: And thus began what went down in history as "The Kitty Royal Rumble".

WRITER'S NOTE: This was the point I vowed never again to put them in the same carrier for any reason, ever.

WRITER'S NOTE: I never imagined the fleeing office cat would pull a 180 at speed, shoot under my armpit and cram himself in the carrier to join the blood-fray. Cats are psychotic beasts.

WRITER'S NOTE: As I checked out, another client came in and saw the bouncing, screaming cardboard carrier "Snooch" was now in. She refused to believe it was a cat and demanded to know what illegal exotic animal I was carrying.

WRITER'S NOTE: And now my child, at last you know, why I don't use one carrier no' mo'.

WELL I WOKE UP THIS MAWNIN'   *Ba-DA-dah-DAH-dah!*
AND I'S IN A BAD MOOD   *Ba-DA-dah-DAH-dah!*
HAD TA HACK UP A HAIRBAW   *Ba-DA-dah-DAH-dah!*
AND WE'S OUT OF GOOSHY FOOD   *Ba-DA-dah-DAH-dah!*

MA WATER DISH EMPTY   *Ba-DA-dah-DAH-dah!*
I'S FEELIN' ABUSED   *Ba-DA-dah-DAH-dah!*
WAGGIN' ANGRY TAIL,   *Ba-DA-dah-DAH-dah!*
I GOTS THE RUSSIAN BLUES, WHOA YEA...

DUN DA DUN DA DUN DA DUDDLE-UN

Take it home, Snooch!

Get your ass back here, you MORON!

But you said...

NOW!!!

WRITER'S NOTE: We had to make this joke, by Federal law.

The lap... the human altar of feline worship, is being desecrated by this infernal Internet Surf Thing Machine.

tappity tappity

Hmm. That tray seems to roll inward.

Now for subtlety!

Dammit, Ebenezer!

kick

YAWN

tappity tappity

Blast!

WRITER'S NOTE: The eternal struggle over lap territory. Will the hostilities never cease?

WRITER'S NOTE: Intelligent and dignified as he may be, Eben is at heart still a cat.

FOUR YEARS LATER

WRITER'S NOTE: The actual version of this involved a cheeseburger being flung into the Venetian blinds in 2000. The cats obsessively licked that same spot until we moved in 2005.

WRITER'S NOTE: Food comes in boxes. Therefore all boxes potentially contain food. J. also operates on this philosophy.
ARTIST'S NOTE: It has served me well.

The theory of Schroedinger's Cat is still debated to this day, whether the cat is alive or dead...

WRITER'S NOTE: My first big fan debate/goofup. Yes, I misspelled Schrödinger. But the argument over whether it's solely quantum mechanics or also a philosophical example of positivism vs. determinism took entirely too long for a JOKE ABOUT CATS.

WRITER'S NOTE: Err... J., you've got a typo up in the—
ARTIST'S FLUB: **I see NOTHING. NOTHING.**

WRITER'S NOTE: I think we all know at least one person to pull this on.
ARTIST'S NOTE: Hey, Mel! I got a great knock-knock joke, but you OW!

WRITER'S NOTE: I've never understood cats' urge to sleep in places that produce the item they loathe most: water.

WRITER'S NOTE: Everyone needs at least one silly hat.

ARTIST'S NOTE: Choo-Choo Bear appears courtesy of Randy Milholland. May his beard grow like the mighty oak.

WRITER'S NOTE: The sad part is this happens at least once a week.

"Nam nyoho ringe kyo..."

"Eben, Mom's not gonna give pettin's while she's asleep."

"I know that, lugnut. Whe had salmon for dinner, so I'm practicing some meditation and aromatherapy."

"Now, while you hold your head over her rising breath, center your thoughts on..."

ZZZNRKTGLMPH! MRGLE!

MPHAAAAAAUGH!

"I didn't want you to stick your whole face in her mouth!"

"But I wanted to find the fishie!"

WRITER'S NOTE: I am never taking Salmon Oil pills again. Just saying.

WRITER'S NOTE: This was half inspired by "Hungry Mungry" by Shel Silverstein, and half by the "Alien Blancmange" sketch from Monty Python's Flying Circus.

WRITER'S NOTE: Inspired by my horror at finding the cats identify the smell of dry-cleaning fluid as "alien cat territory marking".

TEN MINUTES LATER, THE WAR WAS OVER.

AAAAAAAAAAUUUGH!

WRITER'S NOTE: For the record, repeated dry cleaning never gets the smell of cat pee out of non-washable clothing.

WRITER'S NOTE: The only reason I've ever come up with that cats do that "rampant porno pose" for belly rubbins. Or eat bras.

Cave Journal Entry #29: We've made several critical scientific discoveries on our expedition so far. I have discovered that stalagmites make poor scratching posts, while Snooch seems entirely devoted to the study of bats.

Flying mousies!

Now we press on, deeper into the...

RRRRRRRRRRRRRRR...

GREAT SCOTT! Some kind of creature from the abyssal chasm!
FLEE, MY BROTHER!

EEEEEK!

Good lord, guys, it's just the vacuum.

HELP! I'm stuck! Don't eat me! I'm NOT GOOSHY!

RRRRRRRRRRRRRRR...

WRITER'S NOTE: They thought the vaccuum was the most terrifying thing ever. Then I bought a Roomba...

WRITER'S NOTE: I have to say, I adore Tiny Sad Snooch-face.
ARTIST'S NOTE: I really have no idea what happened to his eyes there.

WRITER'S NOTE: This is my theory on how they stay so fat, despite my and the vet's hardest efforts.

WRITER'S NOTE: This is also why I always tip the pizza guys well. Cats just don't tip.
ARTIST'S NOTE: And when they do, you don't want it.

WRITER'S NOTE: Nothing like coming home from a 12-hour day of "GRIPE GRIPE GRIPE" to be greeted with "MEER MEER MEER". I've never done this, but I've been sorely tempted.

WRITER'S NOTE: To be fair, "Snooch" has only ever done one somersault at a time. To be honest, it's still hysterically sad.

WRITER'S NOTE: First they read. Then they get opposable thumbs. Then humanity is doomed.

WRITER'S NOTE: I'll never understand why 30-minute-old water dish contents are "stale" but toilet bowl contents are "fresh".

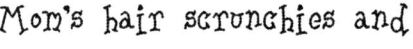
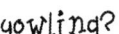

WRITER'S NOTE: "Kitty Opera" is a nightly act at our house as soon as we go to bed. I guess they just want to appreciate the acoustics in private.

WRITER'S NOTE: Mother Nature's answer to self-filling food dishes, if Disney will have you believe it.

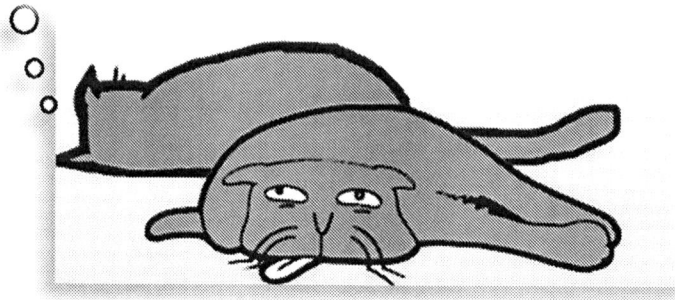

WRITER'S NOTE: Whining burns a lot of calories, you know.
ARTIST'S NOTE: That's how I keep my girlish figure.

...So even if there, for some reason, WERE a horde of lemmings in Mom's living room, they don't act like that. The film company faked it.

The company's run by fake lemmins?

No.

Look. MOVIE company. NOT REAL. Makes the cartoons that you watch? With the giant mouse? Remember?

Giant mousie makes the movies with the cliff jumpin? OHHH! I get it!

Finally!

Great Bast. I give up.

MUST CATCH GIANT SUICIDE MOUSE!

WRITER'S NOTE: I've worked for people who utilized this kind of logic.

WRITER'S NOTE: Similar to the gambling strips, this came from a discussion in NOLA of what "the boys" would be doing.

WRITER'S NOTE: When I moved from Cali to Texas, I had to drive the cats out. I bought some "pet sedatives" that were apparently designed for Great Danes. It was no fun for anyone involved.

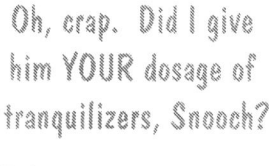

WRITER'S NOTE: Ralph Steadman is a god.
ARTIST'S NOTE: I had so much fun drawing this one.

Oh, my aching... Where are we?

Inna HOTEL!

No, what city? State? Did you see any signs on the drive down?

I saw one that said FOOD!

Serves me right for asking. Go out on the balcony and see if you see any landmarks.

Okey doke! Oooo! Lots of people down there! I's gonna say Hi!

Whatever, moron.

MOW!

CLATTER *CLATTER* **CLATTER**

...death by shinies...

...owie.

Aha! It seems we're on Bourbon Street! Good work there, Snooch!

WRITER'S NOTE: The smell of the Quarter in the afternoon is also a dead giveaway.

Right, now that we know we're in New Orleans, we can assess the dangers we'll face while we're out looking for Mom.

Lucky Dogs?

I meant threats specific to our situation. For example... quick! Behind that luggage cart!

Any hotel employee who sees us will stick us back in the room, so we have to stay hidden on the way outside.

Ready?

CHECK!

DING! RUN FOR IT! *PAF*

Benny? I don't think I can move...

Oh, yes. I forgot about the humidity.

```
WRITER'S NOTE: If you've never had a Lucky Dog... just don't.
ARTIST'S NOTE: How lucky do YOU feel today?
```

WRITER'S NOTE: If you've never had a Hand Grenade (served in the distinctive bottle Snooch has on his head), please do. Just one.

WRITER'S NOTE: Wandering the Quarter at the proper hour will also train you in ninja-level skills of dodging, or ruin your shoes.

Finally got that slime rinsed off. It took a while to find a faucet, but no way was I going to LICK...

Snooch?

Oh, blast.

Where'd he go? Probably someplace shiny or full of food. Like that narrows it down around here.

MOW MOW MOW! MOW MOW MOW MOW!

Eureka! I hope he's not in too much trouble.

 ...CAUSE I GOT CAT CLASS AND I GOT CAT STYLE...

GET DOWN FROM THERE, YOU IDIOT!

CAT STYLE! YEAH! ROCK AND ROLL! WOOOOOOOOOOOO!

```
    WRITER'S NOTE: The Cat's Meow is a fantastic karaoke bar in the
                   Quarter. We had to give mad props.
    ARTIST'S NOTE: What better place to sing like a fool than the French
                   Quarter?
```

I give up. It's too late to convince Mom to go home early. We might as well wait for her in the room.

I wants more fruity ice!

Not on your life. Besides, I need your help with a little "Welcome Back" surprise for Mom.

YAY!

There she is. Keep looking clueless.

Aye-aye!

Hey, guyyshhh, I'm baAAAAAAGH!

THUD

Why'd we string beads across the door?

Since we didn't get to share her vacation experience, I figure she should experience ours... well, mine. I think a hairball on the head should finish off the reven- er, re-enactment. Snooch?

Workin on it! *urk urk urk*

WRITER'S NOTE: It's just not a real tourist experience without someone's vomit.

The poet Carl Sandburg wrote:
"The fog comes in on little cat feet.
It sits looking over the harbor and city
on silent haunches and then moves on."

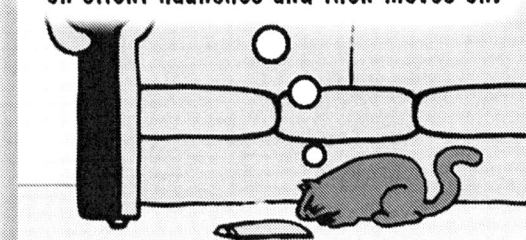

**CRASH!   BANG!
BOOM!   WHACK!**

Christ, Snooch! What's gotten into you?

WHEEEEEEEEEEEEEEEEEEEEEEEE!!!

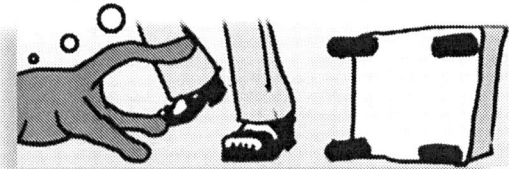

Obviously another brilliant writer's
grasp of reality
sadly lost to Absinthe.

```
WRITER'S NOTE: An old joke from my childhood. I grew up just north of
San Fran, so fog was a constant and the poem was famous. The
thunderous caroming of the cats around the house was a constant
comparison.
```

There you are! No, of course I don't mind watching her. She should have a lot of fun with the boys...

You hear that?

Pizza?

No, you fool, it sounds like Mom's catsitting... and it's a **SHE!**

You said her name's Vera? Okay, you guys have fun tonight!

Wait... a GIRL CAT?

Indeed, my erstwhile brother. We are about to interact, no doubt, with a luscious piece of female felinity! And about time...

KITTIEEEEEEEEEEEEEZ!

She can talk?

IT'S A KID, YOU IDIOT! RUN FOR IT!

```
WRITER'S NOTE: J. and I started dating when his daughter was 1 1/2.
She took to the cats right away. They weren't so thrilled.
```

KITTIES! KITTIES! KITTY KITTY KITTY!

Well, vocabulary isn't one of her strong suits...

She's loud, Eben.

KITTIES ONNA COUCH WIF ME!

Quite loud. But also ideally suited for our needs.

What?

She's a small human, not likely to trip over or step on us. She obviously adores us as the feline gods we are. AND she has opposable thumbs, capable of getting us gooshyfood...

BOUNCY BOUNCY BOUNCY!

...as well as being made entirely of lead, it would seem...

WEEEEEEEE-HEE-HEEE!

```
WRITER'S NOTE: They enjoyed the "someone who pays obsessive attention
   to us and also runs crazily around the house for no reason" part.
```

WRITER'S NOTE: They also counted the Dribble Factor in her favor.

WRITER'S NOTE: She actually did this, as I was watching, when "Eben" licked her foot. Toddlers are the original drama queens.

Okay, Vera, let me show you how to play nice with the kitties...

KITTIES!

Well, at least Mom's realized that we DIDN'T attack the kid. I don't trust it, though.

FLOWER!

See, you pet the kitty nice like this. He likes that!

PET KITTY!

I likes her if I gets the pettins!

I don't know. Perhaps Mom can teach her some manners and tolerability after all.

PET KITTY! PET KITTY!
HOLY- Vera, NO!

Or perhaps I should look into spending the rest of this visit under the couch.

WHAM WHAM WHAM

AaaaaAAAaaaaAA!!!!

WRITER'S NOTE: I think kids gain tactile force recognition around age 5, unfortunately. Poor dribbled cats.

Okay, let's try this again. We brush the kitty with the soft brush, okay? GENTLY.

GENLEEE!

I can't believe you're setting yourself up again, you crumbbrain.

Purr. Purr. But it's the squishy brush! Can't get hurt with that! Purr.

Now you try. Take the brush and... watcha got there, Vera? WAIT, NO--

BWUSH KITTY!!!

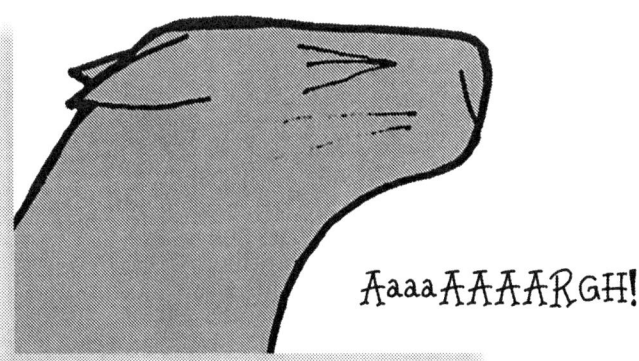

AaaaAAAARGH!

OHMYGODOHMYGOD... Hello, Vet's Office? I need advice on a, uh, extraction...

snicker snrk Say, old chum, did you know you have a toothbrush in your ear?

Sorry. Can't hear you. I have a toothbrush in my ear.

WRITER'S NOTE: Not to mention object subcategories. I'm just glad it wasn't the toilet brush.

WRITER'S NOTE: Fortunately, the boys reacted to gleeful pouncing with frantic wriggling away and hiding rather than Claws-O-Death.

KIIIITIIEEES! I GOTS MILK FOR YOO! HEEEER KITTIES!

YAY! HEEER KITTY!

KITTY GOT MILK NOW!

WRITER'S NOTE: Beware of toddlers bearing gifts. They're usually soggy.

WRITER'S NOTE: Here we entered the 2-year-old "Ih wuz an acc'ident" phase. Like drawing the Pieta in spaghetti on the living room wall is an "accident".

WUMPH!

WRITER'S NOTE: "Snooch" attempted to grab a moth that was about 6 feet up the wall. I think he cleared 6 inches.

WRITER'S NOTE: "Eben's" bird-hunting attempts were also met with much derision.

KNOCK KNOCK KNOCK

Quick! This is our chance to make a break for it! ESCAPE THE CHILD!

RUNNING RUNNING RUNNING

TRICK OR TR...

KITTIES! KITTY KITTIES! KITTIES!

IT'S AN INVASION! RETREAT!

FLEEING FLEEING FLEEING

WRITER'S NOTE: Out of the frying pan...

ARTIST'S NOTE: These were two filler strips while we were down in New Orleans again for the last Presidential Election - a marathon vacation of ten days. I always bring my art laptop on vacation, but after three days in the Quarter during Halloween, my drawing skills were on par with those of an epileptic with Parkinson's disease.

Guys? Vera's gone home, you can come out now...

It's safe now?

In theory. But making her worry for a little while is the second half of her recompense for foisting that child on us.

What's the first part?

I thought apt payment would be all of her cashmere sweaters.

Wow, she just gave 'em all to you?

Well, I wouldn't say "gave," but her entire dry-cleaning hamper is now definitely Mine.

WHAT is that SMELL? AAAAAAUGH!!!

Another reason we should stay under here for a little while longer.

WRITER'S NOTE: I've often wondered why cats invariably express displeasure with anything be peeing on random objects. Then I remember exactly how effective the tactic is.

WRITER'S NOTE: People joke that "cats aren't clean, they're covered in cat spit!" On the other hand, to them we're covered in synthetic rendered cow lard.

Hear the griping of the MEER - Piercing meer!
What a world of misery we portray for you here!
How we whine, whine, whine, In the living room at night!
While we deny that we are fine And on the gooshyfood must dine,
As is our true feline right;
And we kvetch, kvetch, kvetch, That our dinner you must fetch,
With the cacophonic chaos that all cat owners must fear,
From the:

From the whining and the griping of the MEER.

Hear the never-ending MEER, Grating meer!
What a tale of starvation its raucous tones make clear!
Through the balmy darkened air How they ring out their despair!
From the deadened-leaden notes, And off-key,
What a scathing howling floats
To Mom's ears buried 'neath pillows it denotes: Let me be!
Under bedroom door so near,
What a gush of annoyance inhabitants must hear!
How we sneer! How they fear
That their rest is thwarted here
By our perseverance sheer
To the:

Nobody appreciates the classics anymore.

WRITER'S NOTE: Yes, I was an English major. Why do you ask?

WRITER'S NOTE: Cats fail to fathom why you would A. remove traces of their ownership, and B. spend time on anything not devoted to them in the first place.
ARTIST'S NOTE: The text in that strip is completely balls-to-the-wall out of control.

OH NO! She's got the CAT CARRIER! We have to go back to the VET! AAAAAAAA!

That's not the cat carrier, Snooch. Our carrier is smaller than that. Calm down already.

Bigger... it's LUGGAGE! She's goin' away again! Mom's gonna leave us all ALONE! AAAAAAA!

It's not luggage either, you... for Bast's sake, she's doing LAUNDRY. Did you get into the catnip again?

Laundry... washin' things... SHE'S GONNA GIVE US A BATH! AAAAAAAAAAAA!

Is there a doctor in the house?

WRITER'S NOTE: Unlike the 3 AM Crazies, Random Paranoia can last all afternoon, resulting in lacerated ankles and the cat firmly lodged under an armoire.

WRITER'S NOTE: With the boys, it'd be "The Incredible Aw, Forget It, What's To Eat Around This New Place?"

WRITER'S NOTE: Texas fall is lovely, for the entire six hours it lasts.

WRITER'S NOTE: All my cats so far have lived to be between 18 and 21, so I was shocked to find the vet's office referring to the then-7 year old boys as "senior felines". I figured maybe they just needed chalupas.
ARTIST'S NOTE: *Caliente!*

Hey, boys! I'm home from the store! *SLAM*

Egads, that's a lot of food. I'm amazed she carried all that.

FOOD FOOD FOOD OH BOY OH BOY FOODY FOOD FOOD!

Down, Snooch.

Ah, it's **THAT** time of year again. That explains the masses of groceries.

IT'S AS BIG AS *ME!*

Probably so there's no way you can cram it in your mouth.

Aha! A CHALLENGE!
I'm getting the video camera for this.

WRITER'S NOTE: Never eat anything bigger than your own body mass... unless you're Snooch.

WRITER'S BLOCK: The "Playin' the Kitty Cello" pose will never cease amusing me.

WRITER'S NOTE: On the other hand, it couldn't be any worse than Tofurkey.

The fearsome jungle cat stalks through the foliage.

Truly this magnificent creature is king of all he surveys.

He approaches his personal watering hole and is aghast! Some foreign creature has dared to sully his royal sanctuary! The noble animal is rightly outraged!

Don't give me that look, cat. This is MY bathroom. You can just deal with it.

The mighty panther is irked at the violation of his peaceful drinking experience. he plans his revenge.

```
WRITER'S NOTE: I think every cat secretly believes they're truly an
    ocelot deep down. Like an Inner Child with fangs.
```

The fierce jungle felines stalk their natural prey through the dense foliage. They are wily and fearsome!

RARR!

They spot their prey on the plains, and spring! The poor flatlands creature has no chance to escape!

GRR!

There, now don't you feel ferocious? Validated in your felinity?

Hmmmm. No.

Hey! What the heck did you do to my slipper?!

```
WRITER'S NOTE: I suspect they actually created the New Age movement
       just so they wouldn't feel alone in their theories.
```

WRITER'S NOTE: My Mom refers to the boys as "The Grandkittens". I think it's a good compromise.

WRITER'S NOTE: DDR was created around the typical scenario of dodging a cat who wants to "help" you play a video game.
ARTIST'S NOTE: Except when I play it, as a two-hundred pound bald guy stomping like an elephant doing the Watusi is enough to make any cat flee in terror.

Now, now. She seems like the overly-doting type. And since Mom doesn't have kids, all her instincts to spoil grandchildren will go to us.

See, the showering of treats and gooshyfood begins already.

```
WRITER'S NOTE: My Mom is actually nothing like this, except for being
          a Knitting Ninja. A Knitja, if you will.
          ARTIST'S NOTE: You didn't fall far from the tree.
```

Maybe she's just holding out on us. You distract her, I'll snoop through her suitcase.

She's got yarn.

She scares me.

Ooooo!

Yarn, yarn, yarn, dentures, girdle... drat. Looks like we won't be lavished with treats after all.

I have another prezzie for you, Snurchie!

Huh? HEY! AAAAAAAUGH!

Fine diversion there, Snurch.

NEVER AGAIN!

WRITER'S NOTE: As a Knitja myself, I've been tempted to make humiliating things for the boys on occasion. It's just never been worth the resulting bloodshed and poop-on-a-rope.

So, let me try to put this in a timeline. You went through Grandma's luggage and found some "yummy minty stuff," which turned out to be her denture cream?

Mmm hmm.

And after chowing down, you got into her yarn stash and had your typical apoplectic playing fit, correct?

Mmm hmm.

And you still can't figure out how you ended up this way, Tut-Kat-Ahmen?

Nuth-uh!

WRITER'S NOTE: Consequences? What is this alien word you fling at me?

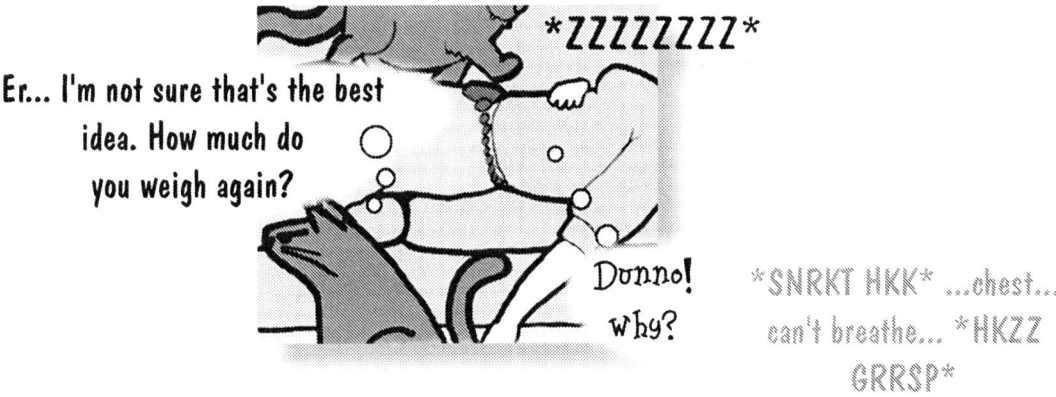

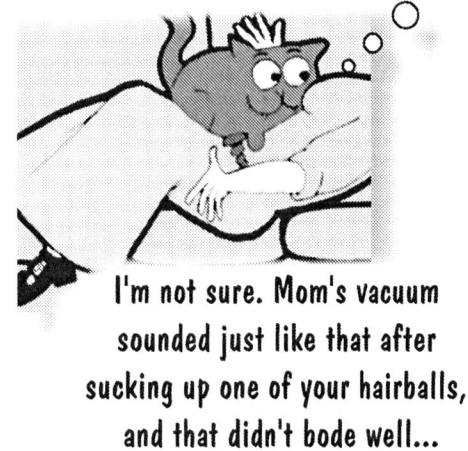

WRITER'S NOTE: "Snooch" isn't quite heavy enough to collapse a lung yet. Don't tell him though, or he'll have something to shoot for.

WRITER'S NOTE: I take it back. My Mom does have a warped sense of revenge.
ARTIST'S NOTE: Single-malt scotch. Eeeegh.

SLAM
Hey, guys! Check out what I got!

A TREE???

Either Mom's taken up indoor forestry or the holidays are here.

I found this great cut-your-own tree farm! It's so much more NATURAL than buying it pre-cut!

Great. Natural dead needles all over, natural terrifying scents of outdoor predators...

AAAAAUGH!

...Natural infestations of the local fauna...

IT'S A TREE PINATA! THIS IS TOO COOL!!

WRITER'S BLOCK: On the first day of Xmas, my Spruce Fir gave to me: A screaming case of heebie-jeebies!

WRITER'S NOTE: Tree by Admiral Ackbar Industries.

Ah, Mom's put out the presents at last. And a fine haul of swag it seems to be.

I wouldn't make any bets, in your case.

How do we know if they're good stuff?

We don't. That's the whole point. Although I make it policy to "mark" anything that doesn't smell like catnip or tuna.

WHEE! Presents are FUN!!!

HORAY!

Tell you what, you can have ALL the ribbon from our presents, and I'll just settle for the stuff inside.

Blessed are the easily amused.

```
WRITER'S BLOCK: Be honest, who hasn't pulled this on younger
                siblings/cousins/nieces/nephews/etc.?
```

Sooooo full. Tummy bursting. Oog.

I'm not surprised. It's impressive that you managed to down two gallons of egg nog and half a case of gooshyfood in one sitting.

Perhaps I should notify Guinness.

I think I'm gonna nap right here for a month.

Do you recall that I said these were the HoliDAYS? Note the plural?

We gotta hustle, guys! People will be here for New Years any minute!

OH NO.

Bwa ha ha. Now we get to see if you can squeeze your bloated carcass under the couch. This should be classic.

WRITER'S NOTE: For this arc, I took a page from Bobbins as well as several other comics, and raised funds for our first toy run by auctioning off a guest appearance.

WRITER'S BLOCK: The winner got both an extended guest appearance, as well as all the original art created for the arc.

WRITER'S NOTE: If they'd known they'd be stuck doing the peepee dance with Snooch on their head, people might not have bid as highly.
ARTIST'S NOTE: Cavy-hat Emperor.

...No, that bathroom's out of order.

But I think there's someone in there.

HEY! HELP! I'M STUCK IN HERE!

Oh, thank Bast...

WHAT? Oh, no...

THANK GOD! Get me out of here!

WHOAAAA...

SOMEONE GET THIS THING OFF MY HEAD!

WEE-HA! RIDIN' HUMAN!

New Year's Resolution: Learn to work a video camera. I could be making a mint off of this.

WRITER'S NOTE: Then again, they might have bid a lot more. People are weird.

The Night Elf Hunter surveys the woods, her fierce feline protector by her side.

All seems quiet, but the giant cat senses something is amiss in the night.

Suddenly, an attack! A vile Orc soldier has invaded the Alliance lands!

AGH! Guys, I'm trying to play World of Warcraft here.

Curse you, Horde scum.

ZUG ZUG!

```
    WRITER'S NOTE: I actually own a "Don'cha wish your girlfriend was
           horde like me" shirt. Addicted? Just a smidge.
    ARTIST'S NOTE: Lord, I drew this before Mel got me into WoW.
Considering I killed my account last Jan. with a level 60 Troll Rogue
        as my main… this strip is from ancient history now.
```

WRITER'S NOTE: More than a tiny nod to the flagpole scene from "A Christmas Story", which is still one of my favorite movies.

Poetry Corner with SNOOCH

"An Ode to Eating", by ME!

A corn chip, a lint wad, a stepped-upon bug,
A wad of old chewing gum stuck in the rug,
Some rotting newspaper once used to wrap meats,
Just some of the many things I loves to eats!

Some glue sticks, a houseplant, and rotting fish guts,
Shoelaces, roadkill, and cigarette butts,
Stray balls of hair and some foil made of tin,
And if I gets sick I'll just eats it again!

WRITER'S NOTE: I didn't realize I was subconsciously filking "My Favorite Things" from The *Sound of Music* until I'd finished the first verse. Then I just ran with it.

The massive gargoyle sits motionless on his perch. For centuries he has watched over the sacred building below.

His eternal duty is to guard against all who would defile the sacred grounds, and his fierce stare never wavers.

I SEEEEE YOOOOOOUUU...

DO YOU MIND???

WRITER'S NOTE: It's always nice to know that cats annoy each other just as much as they do humans.

WRITER'S NOTE: This actually was inspired when J. was sick with a chest cold. After slathering himself with Vapo-Rub, he fell asleep on the couch. Only to awaken to "Snooch" trying to burrow into his chest like a rabid mint-seeking mole.

ARTIST'S NOTE: That cat is a menace to anything minty. Screw catnip, he wants Crème de Menthe.

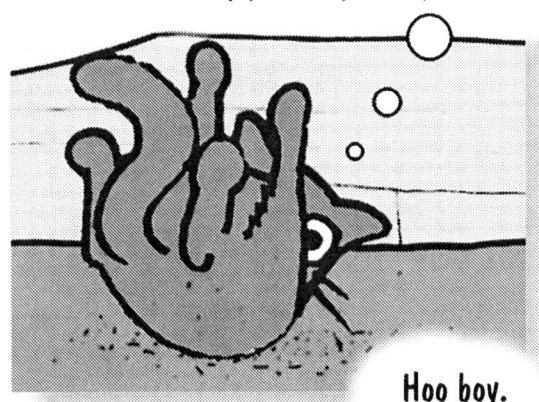

WRITER'S NOTE: Dedicated to all those people we knew in high school who "scored some sweet weed, man! It's from Amsterdam, that's why it smells different!"

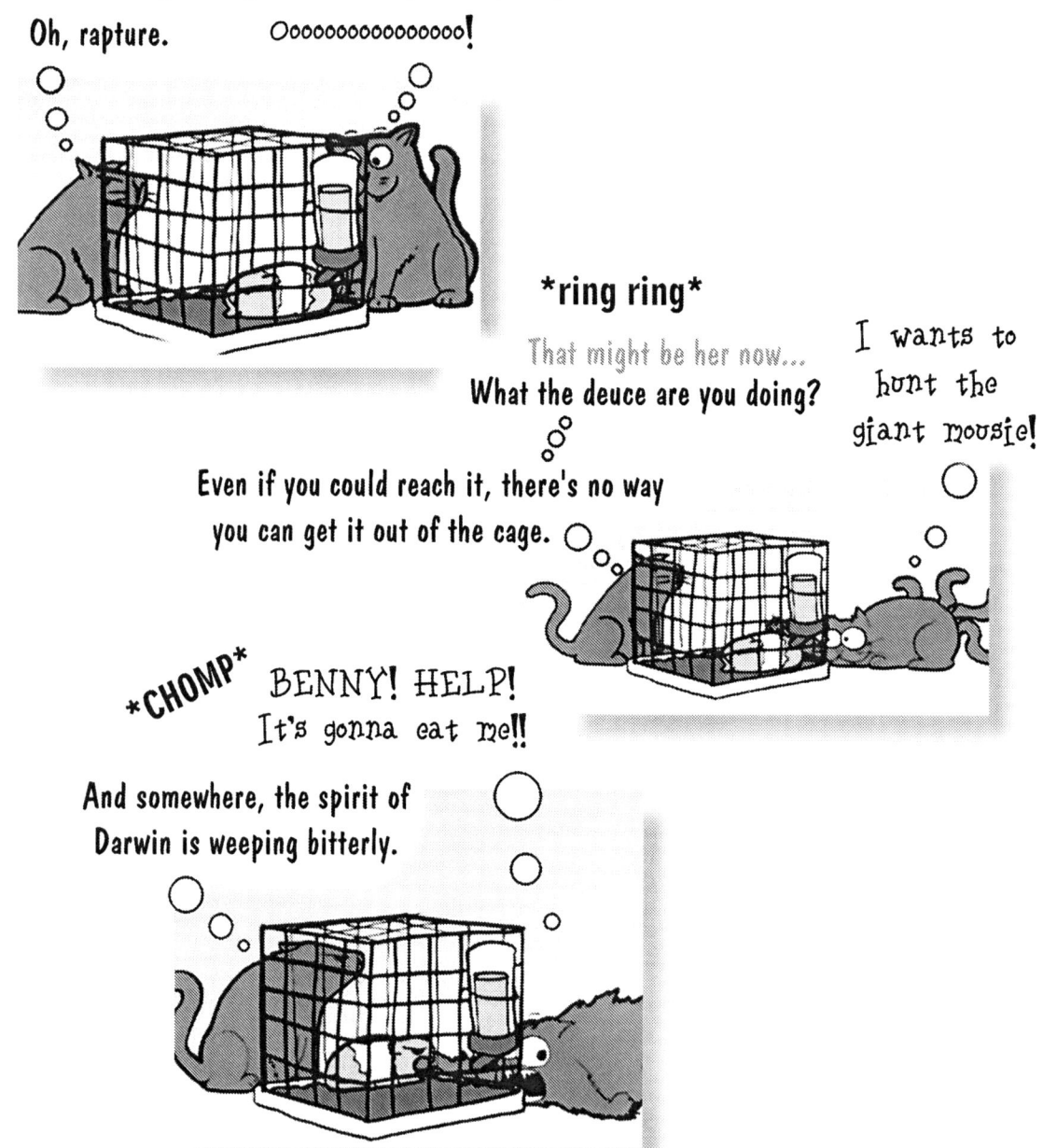

WRITER'S NOTE: I had a guinea pig named Spike when I was a kid. Usually he was an adorable, wurbling little beanbag.

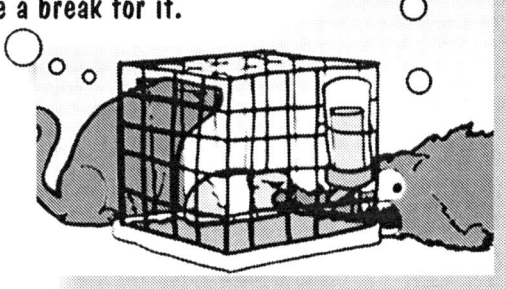

WRITER'S BLOCK: Then occasionally he'd get peeved and turn into the Killer Rabbit from *Monty Python and the Holy Grail*.
ARTIST'S NOTE: WTF is with Guinea Pig lifespans, anyway?

What're we gonna do, Eben?

Go to the kitchen and find something to bribe it with. Lettuce, carrots...

GOOSHYFOOD.

It can TALK?

OF COURSE I CAN, YOU MEATLOAF. IT'S JUST USUALLY NOT WORTH TRYING TO TALK TO CREATURES WHO THINK WITH THEIR STOMACHS. NOW MAKE WITH THE GOOSHYFOOD OR I TURN YOUR BROTHER INTO A MANX.

But gooshyfood's made of meat... kind of. I thought guinea pigs were vegetarian.

IF YOU WANT PROOF, YOUR TAIL IS PRETTY JUICY.

SNOOCH. KITCHEN. NOW.

I'm going, I'm going!

```
WRITER'S NOTE: I don't think he ever developed an actual craving for
                human flesh, but you can never be sure.
ARTIST'S NOTE: How did an animal that will keel over and die for no
          reason ever become a popular CHILDREN'S pet?
```

WRITER'S NOTE: The only pet that isn't planning a world revolution is chihuahuas. They're too busy trying to stay warm and keep out of fast food commercials.

WRITER'S BLOCK: I'm amazed at how a 20-pound cat can throw himself 5 feet in the air when motivated by refracted sunlight.

WRITER'S NOTE: They've never gotten themselves caught in the fan, but I've had to buy stock in canned air from the sheer amount of fuzz that accumulates in my case every month.

ARTIST'S NOTE: Your PC case has more fans than the Dallas Cowboys. Which isn't saying much. OH SNAP.

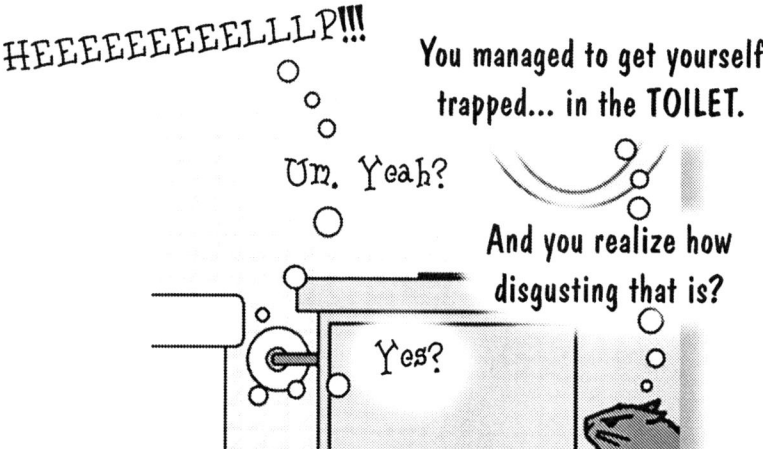

WRITER'S NOTE: I'd just like to note that I'm writing these at 11 PM on a Friday night. My life for you, fans! Bumpitty-bumpitty-bump!

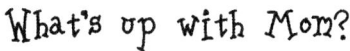

WRITER'S NOTE: I suppose cats' idea of medical therapy does work, in the sense that you realize imminent suffocation is a bigger problem than a simple lung infection.

ARTIST'S NOTE: When I get sick, I tend to become reclusive. Now I can't sleep on the couch without cat hair in my sinuses. When I get a cold, I now sleep in the attic.

What's this thing?

It would appear to be some kind of combination laptop carrier and briefcase on wheels... corporate luggage, if you will. Interesting.

Ooooo, there's a LAP in there?

No, it's a... nevermind. But I find it fascinating that humans have developed an entirelynew carrier layout just for work tedium. Pockets for cell phones and pagers, straps to secure computers...

And dangly toys! WHEEEE!

CLICK

Oops. Um. What do we do now, Benny?

Hush. I'm trying to figure out a way to kill you with a PDA.

```
WRITER'S NOTE: Entirelynew? Doubleplus ungood!
ARTIST'S NOTE: I SEE NOTHING. NUH. THING. GUH.
```

Would you calm down already? Throwing a fit on the electronics and setting everything off isn't going to help. We have to wait until Mom gets...

MUST GET FREEEEEEE!

Here she is!

Work's paging me ALREADY? Heck with them... I'll stash everything in the trunk until I get to the office.

Now what, Eben?

Now I get as far into a corner as possible and you get to show Mom if her laptop is carsick-proof.

WRITER'S BLOCK: One of my childhood cats actually stowed away in the car trunk once when my mother was going to a Gifted teaching class. The planned class schedule went out the window in favor of Mass Cat Calming.

WRITER'S BLOCK: How long would it take to mark all new territory in a 4-story office building? The world will hopefully never know.
ARTIST'S NOTE: We should send that one to Mythbusters.

Snooch? Where'd you run off to? Blast, I hope he hasn't gotten himself stuck in an air duct or anything.

...Again.

WAAAIIIEEEEEEAAHHH!

Great Scott! Snooch! I'm coming, hang on!

So. You found the office break room.

AIIIEEERGH!!!

Did you drink an ENTIRE CARAFE of coffee?

GAHOOGY HOO!

This should be fun.

WRITER'S BLOCK: "Gahoogy hoo!" has apparently become the battle cry of caffeine addicts everywhere, myself included.
ARTIST'S NOTE: The original Too Much Coffee art, sadly, did not look good on a shirt.

WRITER'S NOTE: The desktop behind him, of course, is hosed.

WRITER'S BLOCK: A childhood cat used to try to sneak up on birds with his butt sticking up above the grass. He never could figure out how they could spot him when his eyes were so obviously covered.

WRITER'S NOTE: Hands up, anyone who hasn't done this. Just so I know who the blatant liars are.
ARTIST'S NOTE: This strip has become one of the more popular animated Livejournal icons thanks to some unknown, plucky fan.

Hey, Eben! This chair's all spinny!

For Bast's sake, just leave it alone! We only have to stay hidden for a few more minutes until Mom gets back, so just--

WheeeeEEEeeeEEEeeeEEE!!!

CRASH BONK TINKLE THUD   THAT. IS. IT.

What in the... BOYS???

Uh... hi, Mom!   About time. I was about to resort to using your desk drawer as a litterbox.

WRITER'S NOTE: This also works on coworkers and trainees, for those of you taking notes.

Whew! I don't know how you guys got to the office with me...

YAY! Home at last!

For once, I fully agree. That was an adventure I'm loathe to repeat.

Aww, but I'm gonna miss all the toys there.

Oh, I know I'll be getting at least one more laugh out of that bird-sized desk magnet.

What's that mean?

AAAAAAAAAAAAAAUGH!!!!!!!!

WRITER'S NOTE: Random continuity, you are my special friend.
ARTIST'S NOTE: Randy Milholland has ruined those last two words forever for me. Long story. I can still hear his voice in my brain...

WHAT'S WRONG WHAT'S WRONG WHAT'S WRONG?!?

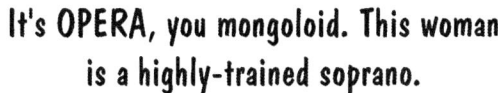

WRITER'S NOTE: Thanks to this strip, I found we have a surprising number of trained singers in our fanbase.

Is the vaccuum gone now?

Yes, it looks like Mom's finally done with all the spring cleaning. She even left us some gooshy food.

Watch it, she also-

WAAAHAAAHAAAGH!

...waxed the kitchen floor.

Owie. I am one with the food dish.

Good thing the tile's clean enough to eat off of.

```
WRITER'S NOTE: No matter how much they watch Jeff Gordon, cats simply
                  can not corner worth a darn.
```

WRITER'S NOTE: J. drew and wrote the first three panels, then challenged me to come up with a punchline. I like a challenge.
ARTIST'S NOTE: And I like PIE!

WRITER'S NOTE: This one, on the other hand, was when I was down with the flu and J. had to come up with a strip at the eleventh hour.
ARTIST'S NOTE: Everyone seems to think all the macabre and dark strips are by me. Strips like this only further that rumor.

WRITER'S NOTE: I LEARNED IT FROM YOU, OKAY MOM?! I LEARNED IT FROM WATCHING YOU!!

WRITER'S NOTE: For those of you who don't live in the South: the roaches here are large enough to require license plates.

We've got to think of something before Mom sees the...

AAAAAAAAGH! OHMIGOD PHONE EXTERMINATOR NOW NOW NOW!

...roach.

All right, I have a plan. Jump down on top of it and crush it with your bulk.

Benny, I'd be ridin' it like a pony.

Good point. This may be a problem even your flab can't handle. We may be doomed.

KNOCK KNOCK KNOCK

Someone called for a Texas roach removal?

What do you know. Cavalry.

YAAAAY!

WRITER'S NOTE: This is a nod to J.'s original comic, FLEM!
ARTIST'S NOTE: Did this right when I was re-launching that series. It didn't take.

WRITER'S NOTE: Did I say I love unexpected continuity? I really, REALLY love it.
ARTIST'S NOTE: WE C WUT U DID THAR

AFTERWORDS

Again and again, we're asked a question at convention panels about comics. The same question every time, usually within the first ten minutes of questions from the audience:

How did you come up with the idea for your comic?

Let's put this one down in writing!

I did a webcomic (started back in late 1998) called FLEM comics. It was mostly Far Side style single panel gags and puns. It got a few hundred readers. Then I started, as many of you remember, a plotline-driven comic called The Jay Series in 1999. My original intent was to do 100 strips about a goth punk from Southern California moving to Dallas, and all the quirks such a transplant entails.

The next thing I knew, four years had passed and I'd done five hundred strips in that story arc. I'd gained a reputation as a mediocre artist with scathing, dirty, disgusting humor. This was not a reputation I found disagreeable - being the Sid Vicious of online comics made me feel happy in the trousers.

But lord, I was so sick of comics when I finally put an end to that series. There were so many other things I wanted to do:

- Write novels
- Do serious art
- Have a life
- Take up macramé
- Learn the fine art of Fish Hammering

As I was to discover, comics get in your blood like some kind of incurable disease. But we'll get back to that.

Mel and I met because of the Jay Series. She was from Northern Cali and could relate to a lot of the humor. And, I would like to note, the first time we met was at a local goth club - she was wearing a chainmail bikini.

Immediately after, she showed me that she did, in fact, own a dress identical to one I'd put on one of my comic characters. This blew me away. I thought I'd invented the design, but there she was wearing it.

Some things are simply meant to be.

We started dating as I completed my first novel, and not long after I moved in with her. And that's when the nagging monkey on my back started hammering on my brain with its greasy, nasty little simian fists.

Mel's cats were (and still are) a pair of Russian Blues named Caramon and Raistlin, after the characters from the Dragonlance novels. Fitting to their names, Caramon is fat and stupid, and Raist is skinnier and crafty as hell.

Watching these damned cats, part of my mind insisted I could be doing something. I *should* be doing something. It was a niggling, horrible fascination - the same kind that doubtless hounded B. Kliban, Jim Davis, George Gately, and many other comic artists who do strips about cats.

And Lord, they are *legion*. I would rattle off a list of twenty or so here, but I don't think I need to - on the web and in print, cats have been a focal point of comics for nearly half a century.

I don't like being unoriginal, so I fought this concept hard. How could I possibly do a new, interesting comic strip about a cat? Or two cats? Or (and you are quite lucky I never ran with this) a herd of mutant cats living in a bombed-out city after World War Three?

And so it came to pass that Mel and I were in Reno playing a game of 21 and losing slowly while getting drunk. The dealer had a four showing, and I had a pair of queens. When I tipsily asked the dealer to split them, everyone within a thirty foot radius gave me a look like I had just announced that I enjoyed molesting Barbary apes.

"You're a damn idiot!" my girlfriend cried, and kicked me in the shin.

"Yes, you are," said the dealer.

So I chose to stay. (As it turned out, the dealer busted anyway and I would have WON THAT SPLIT BUT NEVER YOU MIND.)

I giggled, and when Mel raised a querulous eyebrow, I said:

"That sounded like a conversation your cats would have had."

And she agreed. We even did funny little voices out loud.

Then we moved to the Roulette table, and the voices followed us. "I wants to bet the Oooooooo!" I said, sending us into more giggles. The croupier gave us very strange looks indeed.

Thus it was that, our first night home from that vacation, Mel and I stayed up far too late in bed, staring at the ceiling and coming up with basic concepts for a comic strip. She would do the website, I would do the strips.

Sketched out the character designs the very next day. Registered a site on Keenspace (now Comicgenesis) and Mel started the template process. By the time it launched, I had nine strips drawn, all the time in the world to get more done, and we'd run it up the flagpole and see who saluted. Cat comics HO! I was energized and ready and back in the saddle again!

Five weeks later, I was screaming and throwing things at the cats. I freakin' *hated* cats, *hated* comics, *never wanted to do another strip again*. Put bluntly, I was out of ideas. Cats gambling, making fun of Garfield… yep. That's all I had.

When I mentioned this to Mel, she once again gave me that look. Then she pointed out that she was a writer, loved comics, and would gladly take over the writing. All I had to do was the art.

Now here we are, years later, world famous. Holy crap.

The situation has worked out well. I doodle at work, bring the drawings home and make the strip per her scripts. She doesn't have to do anything but write funny things three times a week.

That's not to say it's been a free ride. I forced her to marry me in 2005, much to the lamentations of everyone we knew. When this strip started, my kid was just getting ready to go pre-school - now Trin's in first grade.

We had an apartment when it all started, now we have a house. We both had car payments, and now those cars are paid off. Gas was $2.78 a gallon when this all began, Bush was in the White House, the Iraq War was going on, and LOST was on ABC.

Okay, some things haven't changed. It hasn't been THAT long.

It is with undying gratitude to Mel's brain that I do these strips. That's all I'm trying to say. She's stuck in like a trooper much to everyone's delight.

On a final note, I'd just like to say that putting this book together has been an insane, dirty, hellish chore. I lost the first 163 hi-res strips due to a hard drive crash, so everything in this book had to be created basically from scratch. I just realized I'm typing in a manuscript that is the culmination of EIGHT SOLID MONTHS OF WORK. Every free moment, every spare minute has been spent re-doing strips I hadn't even looked at in a guinea pig's age. It boggles my mind that (barring the start of the next collection) I can now move on to other things.

Time to find my mallet and a trout. Fish Hammering takes practice, and it's about time I tried something new.

J. Grant, Oct. 2007

When we first started the comic, we didn't think it was going to end up going anywhere.

Okay, I lie. J. is the kind of person who is confident, 24/7, that everything will work out in a way to propel him to fame, fortune, and eventual domination of the universe. I, on the other hand, am usually the reserved and pragmatic one. I write, he draws. He cooks, I brew beer. We tend to balance each other out rather well.

But it also means that I'm still in a rather constant state of shock over where the comic is today. Good shock, the *Holy cow I just won the lottery and discovered a cure for cancer* kind rather than the *Oh my god my house has been infested with flesh-eating parasites* type of shock. It hits me every time we go to a convention, every time we do a panel, every time I look at the hit logs, every time J. goes "Hey, here's the final draft of our first comic compilation. You got an afterword?"

I don't mean to get all Sally Fields-ish "You REALLY like us!" gloopy on you all. But I do have to say that doing this comic and watching it grow, watching people laugh over "Avenge the butt!" or "Giant Suicide Mouse" is one of the most awesome things I've been a part of in my life so far. I never thought I'd be doing something like this, but as long as we keep making you laugh, I'm thrilled to just keep on truckin'.

And I still can't believe he tried to split a pair of queens.
Mel Hynes, Oct. 2007

WALL OF SHAME

We would like to thank (in no particular order):

Faber Castell for making delicious PITT pens, Jennie Breeden, Randy Milholland, Greg Dean, Scott Kurtz, Josh Lesnick, Jin Wicked, Jerry and Mike, B. Kliban, Gary Larson, Chris Mastrangelo, Adam Thrasher, Chris Crosby and the KEEN folks, Mercedes Lackey, Matt Rosemier, Poppy Z., Neil Gaiman, Ennis and McCrea, Warren Ellis, the A-Kon Staff, the Animefest Staff, the CAPE staff, Gandalf's staff, Beer, Jhonen Vasquez, Mike Tidwell of Obscurity Tattoos, the Wed. Night Crūe, Blake, Debra, Kris Stamp, JASC Software, Blizzard, Aeire, J. C. Graphics of Dallas, Smokey and Jane, Eric Burns, Albert Einstein, Blambot Fonts, Paul Riddell and his luscious wife Caroline, Chastain Veterinary Medical Group, the makers of Softpaws, The Weasel King, Big Mike at the Church, Bast, Charles Schulz, Shel Silverstein, everyone else in our famblies not already named, the two real cats that Eben and Snooch are modeled after, and every single fan we've ever had.

You know who you are.

Mel Hynes is a writer, a web admin, a martial arts master, a knitter, a motorcyclist and an avid fan of comic books and video games. She has skydived, walked in London and plays a mean pinball. Her homebrew beer is the kind God would make.

J. Grant is a cartoonist, novelist, musician and network administrator. He has sat in the Mojave staring at the moon and collects tattoos. Under no circumstances should you accept checks from this man.

Both of them live in wedded bliss with the cats and waste far too much time online.

They are also horrible people who start mosh pits at their friends' weddings, as shown in these photos.

They should be considered armed and sarcastic.

Visit StoneGarden.net Publishing Online!

You can find us at: www.stonegarden.net.

News and Upcoming Titles
　　New titles and reader favorites are featured each month, along with information on our upcoming titles.

Author Info
　　Author bios, blogs and links to their personal websites.

Contests and Other Fun Stuff
　　Web forum to keep in touch with your favorite authors, autographed copies and more!

More from James L. Grant
On the Banks of Lethe
(1-60076-051-1 -$14.95 US)

One day Charles receives a voicemail from a frantic woman who notes all the time they spent together when they were younger. She's coming to Dallas to be with him; and she still loves him. Charles has no idea who she is. This is a story of memory, betrayal, trust, two pennies and a dead man.

StoneGarden.Net Publishing
3851 Cottonwood Dr., Danville, CA   94506

Please send me the StoneGarden.net Publishing book I have checked above. I am enclosing $_____ (check, money order for US residents only, VISA and Mastercard accepted—no currency or COD's). Please include the list price plus $3 per order to cover handling costs ($5 outside of the US). Prices and numbers are subject to change without notice. (Prices slightly higher in Canada.)

Name:_____
Address:_____
City:_____State:_____Zip:_____Country:_____
VISA/Mastercard:_____
Exp. Date and CVS Code:_____ /_____
Please allow 4-6 weeks for delivery.

More from James L. Grant
Digging Up Corpses
(1-60076-092-9 -$7.95 US)

One day Charles receives a voicemail from a frantic woman who notes all the time they spent together when they were younger. She's coming to Dallas to be with him; and she still loves him. Charles has no idea who she is. This is a story of memory, betrayal, trust, two pennies and a dead man.

StoneGarden.Net Publishing
3851 Cottonwood Dr., Danville, CA   94506

Please send me the StoneGarden.net Publishing book I have checked above. I am enclosing $_____ (check, money order for US residents only, VISA and Mastercard accepted—no currency or COD's). Please include the list price plus $3 per order to cover handling costs ($5 outside of the US). Prices and numbers are subject to change without notice. (Prices slightly higher in Canada.)

Name:_____
Address:_____
City:_____State:_____Zip:_____Country:_____
VISA/Mastercard:_____
Exp. Date and CVS Code:_____ /_____
Please allow 4-6 weeks for delivery.